P9-DLZ-360

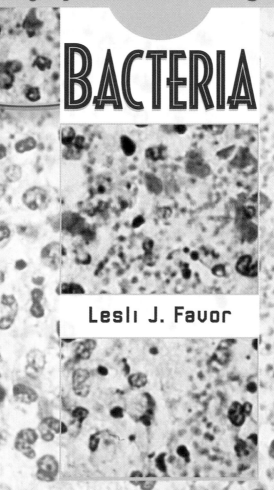

GERMS
The Library of Disease-Causing Organisms™

BACTERIA

Lesli J. Favor

The Rosen Publishing Group, Inc.
New York

Published in 2004 by The Rosen Publishing Group, Inc.
29 East 21st Street, New York, NY 10010

Copyright © 2004 by The Rosen Publishing Group, Inc.

First Edition

Library of Congress Cataloging-in-Publication Data

Favor, Lesli J.
Bacteria/Lesli J. Favor.—1st ed.
    p. cm.—(Germs: the library of disease-causing organisms)
Summary: A study of the single-celled disease-causing micro-organisms known as bacteria, discussing how they function, how they cause illness, and how we can protect ourselves against them. Includes bibliographical references and index.
ISBN 0-8239-4491-3 (lib. bdg.)
1. Bacteria—Juvenile literature. [1. Bacteria.]
I. Title. II. Series.
QR74.8.F38 2004
579.3—dc22

579.3
FAV
c. 1

2003010927

Manufactured in the United States of America

On the cover: A scanning electron microphotograph of rod-shaped *Mycobacterium tuberculosis* bacteria, the main cause of human tuberculosis.

CONTENTS

Introduction

Earth, its bodies of water, and the air above it are teeming with tiny one-celled organisms called bacteria. Scientists believe they are probably the most numerous living things on our planet. The more that is learned in the study of bacteria (called bacteriology), the more it becomes clear that these microorganisms are intricately involved in every life process on Earth, whether that of plant, animal, or human.

Scientists believe that bacteria have been around for 3.5 billion years. Some of the most ancient types, called archaebacteria, lived in ocean bottoms around the hot vents of underwater volcanoes. Since the vast majority of bacteria cannot be seen without the aid of a microscope, these organisms were not "discovered" until the 1670s. In the Netherlands in 1674, Antonie van Leeuwenhoek (1632–1723) was pursuing his hobby of observing tiny things through homemade magnifying lenses. When he observed a drop of water, he noticed "very little animalcules" and made sketches of them. These "animalcules" were bacteria. Leeuwenhoek observed bacteria in scrapings from his teeth, in material taken from human intestines, and in pond water, rainwater, and well water. Later he speculated that animalcules could be transported from place to place on dust in the air.

What Leeuwenhoek did not know was that the microscopic organisms he had found and others like them were the causes of many diseases. Until this time, people believed that diseases and pests sprang spontaneously from the substances in which they were found. Maggots, it was believed, grew spontaneously from rotten meat. Frogs grew out of the muck at the bottom of a pond. Diseases grew from the bodies they afflicted. Called spontaneous generation, this theory was challenged by Leeuwenhoek's idea that microscopic organisms were carried by air or by other means.

But it was not until the 1860s that science took the next big leap in its understanding of disease. French chemist and microbiologist Louis Pasteur (1822–1895) proved that germs cause disease. In further research, Pasteur developed a process, now called pasteurization, to destroy microorganisms in foods and drinks, making them safe to consume. He also experimented with immunizing and vaccinating animals against diseases. Around the same time, in the 1870s and 1880s, German physician Robert Koch (1843–1910) identified the anthrax life cycle and identified the bacteria responsible for tuberculosis and cholera.

Indeed, some of the most horrific plagues and epidemics of human history originated with bacteria.

Leprosy, tuberculosis, and diphtheria are all bacterial diseases. The black death (bubonic plague) that wiped out roughly a third of Europe's population in the fourteenth century was caused by the bacterium *Yersinia pestis*. Another *Yersinia pestis* epidemic swept through China in the mid-nineteenth century, and in the first decade of the 1900s, the bacteria killed 10 million people in India.

The *Vibrio cholerae* bacterium has caused at least half a dozen pandemics since 1784. A pandemic is an outbreak of a disease that affects a wide geographic area and a high proportion of the population. In 1784 in northern India, cholera killed 20,000 pilgrims at Hurdwar, a holy place. During the 1800s, cholera pandemics struck other regions of India and England, France, and Egypt.

Though it is a simple single-celled microscopic organism, a bacterium lives a life that is far from simple. Because of the functions bacteria perform in the human body, they are closely involved in every aspect of every human's life. We'll begin with an overview of these tiny creatures, from their cell structure to their sizes and shapes. Then we'll describe how bacteria live and what their role is in causing disease. Finally, we'll look at some beneficial bacteria and the ways in which they are used to enhance life and preserve the environment.

1 *What Are Bacteria?*

Bacteria are everywhere. They live on and in the human body and the bodies of other living things. They live in dirt, in the air, and in water. Unfazed by extreme temperatures, some types of bacteria live in hot springs, in snow and ice, or in frozen soil. Others thrive in the salty seas and oceans. Still others live high in the upper atmosphere. These unseen inhabitants of the earth and sky are more numerous than any other type of living organism.

Bacteria are classified as part of the kingdom Monera. Organisms in this kingdom have simple cell structures, and most of them are microscopic, meaning they cannot be seen with the naked eye. Besides bacteria, also called eubacteria, Monera include archaebacteria and cyanobacteria. Cyanobacteria were formerly called blue-green algae, but scientists recategorized them after discovering they were more similar to bacteria than to algae.

Cell Structure

Each bacterium is formed of only one cell, which has a very simple structure. Regular cells have a

Cyanobacteria like these are often mistaken for algae, but they are actually an ancient and primitive form of life that is closer to bacteria.

cell wall surrounding the cell's cytoplasm, and inside the cytoplasm are organelles and a nucleus containing genetic material. Bacteria do not have this complex internal structure. In bacteria, all cellular matter floats freely within the cell wall. A few kinds of bacteria do not even have a cell wall.

Bacteria, like other members of the kingdom Monera, are prokaryotes. This means that bacteria do not have a distinct nucleus. Regular cells with nuclei and organelles like mitochondria are called eukaryotes and are considered a later evolutionary development. In contrast, DNA (deoxyribonucleic acid, the genetic material of a bacterium), rather than being contained in a nucleus, floats freely within the cell.

Size

Bacteria are microscopic—so tiny that millions could fit on the head of a pin. A fingernail, for instance, may have tens of thousands of bacteria on its surface. Millions would fit on the surface of a quarter. The period at the end of this sentence has plenty of surface area for 10,000 of these microbes. The rare exception, a so-called huge bacterium found on the ocean bottom near Namibia in Africa, is about the size of the period at the end of this sentence. Scientists were amazed to find it, realizing that it was the first known bacterium visible with the naked eye.

A unit of measurement called a micrometer, or micron (μ), is used to measure bacteria. Twenty-five thousand microns equal 1 inch (2.5 centimeters). Some of the smallest bacteria are only .5 micron in length. It would take 50,000 of them to make a line 1 inch (2.5 cm) long. Most bacteria are between 1 and 5 microns in size. The rare bacteria found off the coast of Namibia can grow up to 500 microns long, a length equaling about 0.02 inch (0.5 millimeter).

Shapes and Movement

Bacteria are grouped into three types of cells based on their shape: spherical, rodlike, and spiral. Coccus cells are spherical. Certain types of cocci cause strep throat and pneumonia, while other types live harmlessly on the human body. Bacillus cells are shaped like rods. Bacilli can cause tuberculosis and anthrax, among other diseases. Spirillum cells have a loose

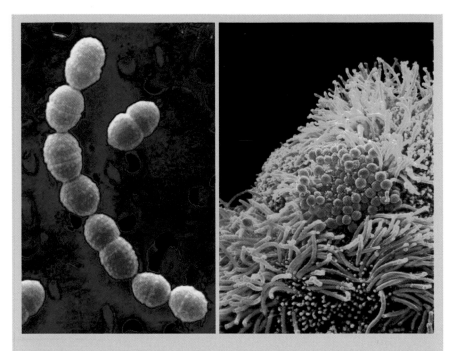

Streptococcus cremoris, at left, is used to add flavor to different kinds of cheese. At right, a colony of staphylococcus grows on the threadlike cilia of the human trachea. These bacteria can cause anything from minor skin infections to fatal pneumonia.

spiral shape. Also called spirochetes, they can cause Lyme disease and other infections.

Most bacteria live alone as single cells. But sometimes bacteria stick together as pairs, clusters, or lines of cells. The prefix "diplo" is used to describe cells clinging together as a pair. For example, a stuck-together pair of coccus bacteria are called diplococcus. *Diplococcus pneumoniae* is one cause of conjunctivitis, an eye inflammation. The prefix "staphlyo" is used to describe coccus bacteria that are together in clusters. Staphylococcus bacteria cause staph infections, meningitis, food poisoning, and other ailments. The prefix "strepto" is used when bacteria cells cling together in chains. Streptococci, for example, are chains of coccus bacteria. Looking much like strings of beads, they cause strep throat, scarlet fever, sinustis, and other infections.

While some bacteria can move themselves about, others are passengers of the substance in which they live. The mobile ones vary in their capabilities. A slimy bacterium can slide slowly along on its own slippery coating. Those with flagella, which are long, whiplike extensions, can propel themselves forward in a swimming movement. Spirochetes use structures similar to flagella, which are located beneath the surface of the cell membrane, to swim about. When sensing danger, such as a toxic chemical, bacteria move away from it. When sensing food, hungry bacteria move toward it. Other bacteria, though immobile on their own, may float through the air on a speck of dust or on an insect, hurl through

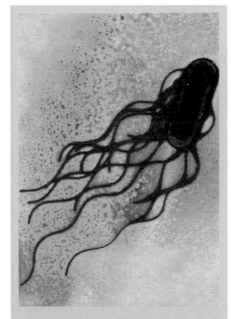

This salmonella bacterium has long flagella to help it move. There are more than 2,000 types of *Salmonella*, but most food poisoning in humans is caused by two kinds, *Salmonella typi* and *Salmonella paratyphi*.

the air in the droplets of a sneeze, or ride along on the skin of an animal.

Reproduction

Bacteria are present all over the earth in such great numbers because of their ability to reproduce rapidly. In a process called binary fission, a bacterium splits in two. Each half then splits in two, and those four parts each split in two. The cell division continues, limited only by available space and nutrients. This is called asexual reproduction. The original cell is called the mother, and the two cells resulting from the split are daughter cells. While at first the daughters are half the size of the mother, they grow.

In favorable conditions, one bacterium can divide as often as once every twenty minutes. For example, if you start with one bacterium at twelve o'clock, you would have two at 12:20, four at 12:40, and eight at 1:00. Bacteria, of course, are present in great numbers. The tip of a finger might hold 10,000 bacteria at 12:00. By 12:20 there are 20,000 bacteria on the fingertip. By 12:40 there are 40,000 bacteria, and at 1:00 there are 80,000. If humans multiplied on this scale, a family of four would be a family of thirty-two in one hour. More commonly, bacteria divide once every two or three hours and others only once every sixteen hours.

While most bacteria grow through binary fission, some grow through conjugation, a sexual process.

In conjugation, two bacteria join and exchange DNA before pulling back apart. While the cells produced by fission are identical to the mother —they are clones—the cells produced by conjugation share DNA from both parents. They are unique.

Occasionally a mutant bacterium appears. It has DNA slightly different from the parent cell's DNA. As a result, the mutant may survive conditions that would kill its parent cell. Researchers believe that mutation is responsible for bacteria's ability to adapt to such a wide array of living conditions, both now and throughout the microbes' long history.

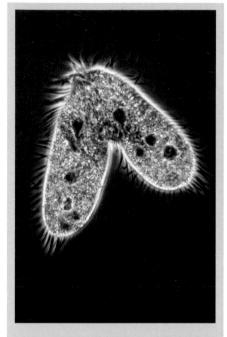

Stylonychia protozoa such as these reproduce by conjugation, a reproductive process used by some bacteria.

2 The Lives of Bacteria

The average life span of a bacterium is anywhere from a few minutes to a few hours long. Like any other living organism, the bacterium survives by inhabiting an environment favorable to its needs, getting adequate nutrients, and avoiding enemies. Besides simply surviving, bacteria carry out a host of activities, depending on where and how they live. While some of these activities are harmful to humans, others are beneficial and even essential to human life.

Habitats

Bacteria live everywhere—in more environments and habitats than any other kind of living thing. Salt water, freshwater, sand, dirt, animals, humans, plants, air, rotting flesh—these are all desirable habitats for bacteria of one kind or another. Scientists studying rocks and dirt in mines cut 1,300 feet (390 meters) deep in the earth find bacteria down there. Others studying air 19 miles (30 kilometers) above the earth's surface find bacteria there, too. Some bacteria survive extreme temperatures, whether freezing or boiling, that would kill other

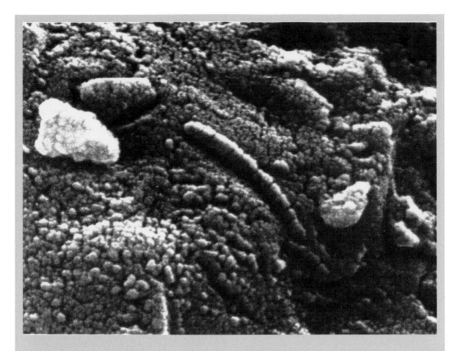

This electron microscope image shows a tubelike form, smaller than a human hair. It was detected in an asteroid found in Antarctica that is believed to come from Mars. Some scientists think it is evidence of primitive bacterial life on Mars.

living things. Some types, called anaerobes, thrive in places with no air. They obtain oxygen from the food they consume. Others called aerobes rely on oxygen-rich air for survival, much like humans and animals. Still others can survive either with or without air.

A few kinds of bacteria form spores. A bacterial spore is a resting stage, making it possible for the cell to survive destructive conditions. Some spores survive in boiling water for hours, while others survive chemical poisons for hours without dying. Other types of spores endure extreme cold or dehydration. With their tough, dry coats, some spores have survived for hundreds of years. The ruins of Rome have yielded spores nearly 2,000 years old. Other spores have stayed alive even longer. Off the coast of California, in the sediment of the Pacific Ocean, spores were found that dated back about 5,800 years. In Minnesota's Elk Lake, sediment yielded spores believed to be the oldest ever found, at around 7,000 years old.

When a spore encounters favorable living conditions once again, the tough coat gives way to a healthy cell wall. The bacterium resumes normal, active life. Moisture, warmth, and nutrients are conditions favorable to reactivating a dormant bacterium.

Certain bacteria live in the rumens, or stomach sections, of some animals. Here they help break down cellulose, the stiff matter in plants, during digestion. Without the aid of these bacteria, cows, sheep, goats, and other animals would receive little nutrition from the green plants they graze on. Humans, too, rely on bacteria to help digest food. Colonies of *Escherichia coli* thrive in the intestines, helping to break down food and release nutrients in usable form for the human body.

The human mouth is a bacterium's paradise. Warm and moist, it provides an ideal habitat for many billions of bacteria. Sugars and starches in food pass through the mouth, feeding the bacteria as well as their host. Colonies of the microbes live on the tongue, teeth, gums, in crevices between teeth, and in the plaque that builds up on teeth.

Most of these microbes in the mouth are harmless. Some are beneficial, while others can do damage. For instance, teeth that remain unbrushed allow bacteria to grow and produce sufficient acid to cause tooth decay. The longer the bacteria colonize the tooth, the deeper into the tooth their acid eats, first through the enamel, then through the dentin of the tooth, and finally into its soft, pulpy center. If bacteria cause this much damage to a tooth, it likely will need to be pulled out by a dentist. In a similar fashion, gums in an untended mouth allow bacteria to multiply and cause gum disease.

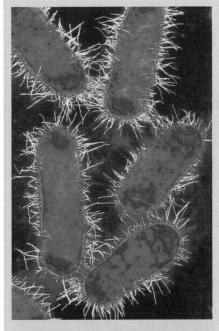

E. coli are usually harmless, but can sometimes overproduce and cause infections. *E. coli* can be passed from person to person or live in under-cooked meat or unpasteurized milk.

Nutrients

Bacteria need nutrients to survive, just like people do. The bacterium takes in food through the cell wall. First, the bacterium secretes enzymes from the cell wall onto food outside the wall. The enzymes break down the food into soluble form. Being soluble means the food can dissolve in a liquid, and in this form the bacterium absorbs the food through its cell wall. Inside the cell, enzymes further process the food.

For some bacteria, mineral compounds provide the best nutrients. Using sulfur, minerals in water, and carbon dioxide from air, these bacteria manufacture carbohydrates, fats, proteins, and vitamins. Because they create their own nourishment, they are called autotrophic, or self-nourishing. Other bacteria need more complex foods. Parasitic bacteria depend on a living host to provide nourishment. Bacteria called saprophytes feast on rotting animal carcasses, dead bugs, and other types of decaying flesh.

Inset: A cross-section of a fusobacterium, which contributes to tooth decay. *Above:* Bacteria gather in a hole resulting from tooth decay.

Just as plants use photosynthesis to manufacture nutrients, so do some anaerobic bacteria. These bacteria contain substances that capture energy from sunlight and use the energy to make food. Whereas plants give off oxygen as a waste product, the anaerobic bacteria do not. Cyanobacteria also use photosynthesis to make food, and these do give off oxygen as waste.

After processing the food, the bacteria expel waste matter through the cell walls. The waste products of some bacteria are poisonous to other living things and are called toxins.

Balance in Nature

One of bacteria's valuable roles in nature is to assist in the decay of dead organisms. Along with earthworms and fungi, bacteria break down organic matter such as fallen leaves, dead plants and wood, and animal carcasses. Bacteria work during the final stages of decomposition, after earthworms and fungi have broken the matter into tiny pieces. As they feast on organic molecules, bacteria break them down into basic elements including nitrates, minerals, water, and carbon dioxide. They release these elements back into the soil and air, where they originated. Thus enriched, the soil and atmosphere can support a new cycle of life. If it weren't for the work of bacteria in decomposition, dead organic matter would pile up, tying up the basic elements needed for new life. Eventually, all life on Earth would die out.

Another part of the decomposition process involves breaking down solid waste from humans and animals. In breaking down manure, for example, bacteria release nitrogen, phosphorus, and potassium,

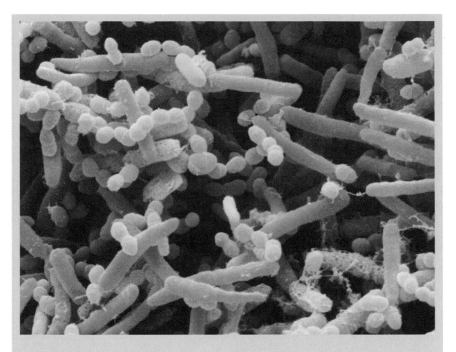

Rod-shaped bacilli and spherical coccus bacteria thrive in compost, which is a mixture of decomposing matter used to improve the quality of soil. Many types of bacteria and fungi help create compost by breaking down plant tissue.

important nutrients in fertile soil. For this reason, decaying manure is used as a soil fertilizer. Every day around the world, billions of pounds of waste are produced. Without the steady work of bacteria, aided by other microbes including fungi and protozoa, the waste would create an unlivable world.

In septic tanks, anaerobic bacteria break down human waste. A by-product of the process is gas, mainly methane, which can be trapped and used as a fuel. The remaining solid matter can be used as fertilizer. On a larger scale, bacteria are used to treat the sewage of huge cities. At sewage plants, huge beds of gravel are sprayed with sewage. On the gravel is a film formed of aerobic bacteria and other microbes. These microorganisms go to work breaking down the waste.

In a process called nitrogen fixation, bacteria in the soil help green plants thrive by making nitrogen accessible. In its gaseous form, nitrogen makes up nearly 80 percent of the air. However, green plants cannot use nitrogen in the gaseous form. They depend on bacteria that take in nitrogen to fuel their own growth. Bacteria such as azotobacter use nitrogen gas to form nitrates and ammonia, compounds that plants use to fuel their growth. Other bacteria called rhizobia live in nodules (swellings) on the roots of legumes such as peas, beans, and clover. In this symbiotic relationship, both the microbe and the plant benefit. From the plant the bacteria obtains food, and from the bacteria the plant obtains nitrogen compounds.

By effecting decay, emitting carbon dioxide, and releasing nutrients into the soil, bacteria help maintain balance in nature. However, bacteria's role in nature is not limited to decay and fixing nitrogen for plants. Some of bacteria's most dramatic activities, at least from a human's perspective, are those involving food or disease. In these areas, bacteria can mean life or death to an individual and even to vast populations.

3 Bacteria, Food, and Disease

Improperly prepared food may deliver harmful bacteria to the consumer, causing varying degrees of sickness. While some bacteria cause food to become inedible or poisonous through spoilage, other bacteria are used to produce healthy, tasty foods such as cheeses and yogurt.

Bacteria active in the decay process are responsible for food spoilage. Moderate temperatures and some moisture are ideal for bacteria to thrive in many types of food. However, refrigeration helps slow the spoilage process, and freezing can halt spoilage, at least until the food is thawed. At this time, the bacteria become active again. Heat used in cooking and baking can kill many types of bacteria.

Bacteria bring about spoilage more readily in some foods than in others. A cheesy slice of pizza left sitting on a kitchen counter will spoil much faster than a piece of dry toast sitting beside it. A glass of milk left out on the counter will sour more quickly than a glass of sugary, acidic lemonade. A can of salt, a box of sugar cubes, a bag of flour, and a box of dry breakfast cereal are all examples of foods that do not readily support bacterial growth. On the other hand, meats, cheeses, and prepared foods are hospitable to bacterial growth, due in part to their moisture content. In general, most types of bacteria do not grow in dry or salty foods. For this reason, drying and salting are effective methods of preserving meats and other foods. Similarly, very sugary foods are not conducive to bacterial growth, nor are acidic foods such as vinegar.

Special care must be taken in the canning of foods. In the canning process, foods are heated to kill bacteria and then sealed in sterile jars or cans. Thus prepared, foods can be stored without refrigeration or freezing for many months. However, some spores and heat-tolerant bacteria called thermophilic bacteria survive high temperatures. If sufficient heat is not used for the proper length of time, the microbes are not killed. They grow in the canned food or become active when the container is opened.

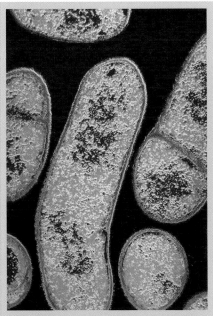

The bacteria *Clostridium botulinium* can cause respiratory failure and paralysis. Botulism victims are unable to breathe properly and may have to be put on a ventilator for several weeks to recover.

Botulin, a poisonous bacterial waste product, causes botulism. Even in tiny amounts, the toxin attacks the human nervous system and can be fatal. Botulin comes from a spore that survives boiling water for up to five hours. Home-canned foods are most susceptible to botulin. Superheated with steam, commercially canned foods are less likely to carry the toxin. Whatever its origin, a swollen can or an unopened jar whose suction seal has popped up is likely to contain botulin.

Pasteurization and Fermentation

Pasteurization is a method of killing harmful bacteria in fresh dairy products such as milk and cream. Milk bottled for sale to the public is pasteurized, as are half-and-half and cream. One method of pasteurizing fresh milk is to heat it for thirty minutes at 145° Fahrenheit (63° Celsius). A quicker method of killing the bacteria is to heat it to 161°F (71.6°C) for fifteen seconds. Immediately following both methods of pasteurization, the milk is cooled rapidly to preserve its flavor. Other methods of pasteurization are used for other dairy products.

The changes wrought by bacteria in food can be a good thing. Fermentation is the key. Fermentation is a chemical process brought about by certain microorganisms, including some kinds of bacteria. For example, *Lactobacillus bulgaricus* bacteria change milk sugar into lactic acid, a process that produces buttermilk, cream, and yogurt. So-called live yogurt contains living lactobacilli. A seemingly endless variety of cheeses are made using different combinations of bacteria, each blend resulting in a different flavor. Other foods made with the help of bacteria include pickles, soy sauce, and sauerkraut.

Hygiene and Cooking

Poor hygiene on the part of food handlers can allow bacteria to find their way into the human stomach and wreak havoc there. Bacteria make up a large part of solid human waste, for example, and a person who does not wash up after a trip to the restroom can transfer bacteria to the food he or she touches. The

Lactobacillus bulgaricus, shown here in pink, produce lactic acid and add flavor to milk and yogurt. They also live in the digestive tract of humans and other animals, where they inhibit some disease-causing bacteria.

contaminated food can cause stomach pain, vomiting, and diarrhea.

Salmonella, rod-shaped bacteria, live in the intestines of chickens and help the fowls digest their food. When chickens are slaughtered and sold as raw poultry, bacteria can survive on the meat. A cook who does not thoroughly wash his or her hands after handling raw chicken can transfer salmonella to cooked food, clean dishes, or anything else touched afterward. Similarly, the cook must prepare the chicken at a high enough temperature to kill the salmonella. Raw or under-cooked eggs are also carriers of salmonella bacteria. Symptoms of poisoning by salmonella include stomach pain, fever, vomiting, and diarrhea.

Other types of bacteria invade the intestines when poor hygiene or inadequate cooking allow them to survive on food. Campylobacter, for example, survives on undercooked food. Once in the intestines, this bacteria begins destroying the mucus lining, causing diarrhea. Shigella is a kind of bacteria carried by flies and found on food. Poor sanitation in food preparation can allow shigella to survive and attack the lining of the small intestines. Symptoms include cramps and diarrhea, the body's way of trying to rid itself of the microbe.

Disease

While some bacterial infections are food-borne, others result when bacteria invade the body by other

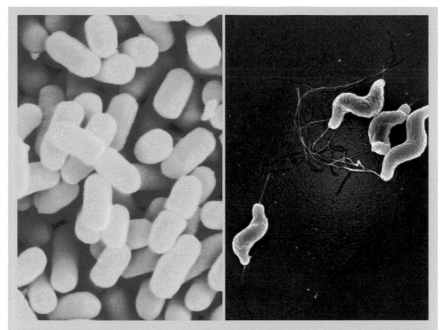

These *Shigella sonei* at left can cause shigellosis. It can be passed from person to person through hand contact, food contamination, or even swimming pools that aren't properly chlorinated. At right, *Campylobacter jejuni* are usually spread through cutting boards or knives that have been used on infected raw meat and have not been washed before being used on other foods.

means. Called pathogens, disease-causing bacteria are responsible for infections ranging from acne to pinkeye to pneumonia. Some pathogens multiply in the body so rapidly that they interfere with the functions of tissues and organs. Others excrete toxins, chemicals that are poisonous to the human body.

The human body has natural defenses against the entry of disease-causing bacteria. On the skin's surface, harmless bacteria live, protecting their turf against invading bacteria. Mucous membranes and tiny hairs in the nose trap bacteria, where they are expelled when the nose is blown. Bacteria entering through the mouth or nose may be killed by mucous membranes in the mouth or throat. Those making their way to the stomach are killed by acids there. Tears in the eyes and saliva in the mouth form additional defenses.

Cuts, scrapes, skin punctures, and animal bites provide pathways for bacteria to enter the body. But even these temporary entryways are protected. When the skin is cut, for example, some of the damaged cells release histamine. This chemical signals the body to send more blood to the injury, and the area swells. The blood clots, sealing the cut. Besides that, white blood cells rush to the injury. Called phagocytes, they eat invading bacteria. Afterward, the phagocytes die, and the mass of dead phagocytes and demolished bacteria remains as pus. Other immune system white cells called lymphocytes produce chemicals to attack and kill bacteria and other invaders. Specific lymphocytes target specific kinds of bacterial invaders. Despite the body's defenses, some pathogenic microbes find a way in and survive. Once inside the body, the bacteria carry on with the business of living—multiplying, eating, and excreting waste. Infections result when they multiply to numbers great enough to interfere with bodily functions or when their poisonous waste products—toxins—cause damage.

Pneumonia is a respiratory infection resulting from bacteria that multiply rapidly in the lungs. As the lungs become filled with bacteria, the person has increasing difficulty breathing. Eventually the victim can suffocate and die.

Hemophilus bacteria are mostly harmless, except for *Hemophilus influenzae*, which causes whooping cough and meningitis. Whooping cough, characterized by coughing and vomiting, is highly contagious. Meningitis is an inflammation of the membranes covering the brain and spinal cord. Meningitis is also caused by other bacteria, including meningococci and various kinds of pneumococci, streptococci, and staphylococci. Most frequently, children under the age of ten suffer from the disease. Early diagnosis is vital since brain damage and death may result.

A soil bacterium, *Clostridium tetani,* lurks in spore form, entering scratches or puncture wounds that are contaminated with dirt. Once in the wound, the spore is activated by rotting tissue. It releases a toxin that enters the nervous system and spinal cord, causing

Leprosy, or Hansen's disease, causes the skin to go numb and grow nodules and lesions. It can be treated with a combination of several drugs, but there is not yet a cure.

These Russian prisoners are being treated for tuberculosis, or TB. TB is caused by *Mycobacterium tuberculosis* bacteria and is spread through inhaling airborne droplets from an infected person. It causes small tumors to grow and damage the lungs. If not treated, it can sometimes spread to other organs or cause death.

tetanus. Also known as lockjaw, a tetanus infection causes severe, uncontrollable muscle contractions. Spasms of the jaw muscles give the disease its nickname. The disease can be fatal, though it is preventable with a vaccine.

The list of bacterial infections goes on. *Streptococcus* causes scarlet fever. *Mycobacterium bovis* causes tuberculosis. Carried by ticks, *Borrelia burgdorferi* causes Lyme disease. *Rickettsiaceae* causes typhus and spotted fever. The *Chlamydia trachomatis* bacterium causes chlamydia, a sexually transmitted disease that can result in the inability to have children.

Leprosy, more common in centuries past but still present today, results from *Mycobacterium leprae*. *Legionella pneumophila* causes Legionnaire's disease, a kind of pneumonia. Found in refrigerated foods such as potato salad and cold cuts, the bacterium *Listeria monocytogenes* causes food poisoning and, in some cases, death.

Not all pathogens and toxins are life threatening. For instance, acne is a bacterial infection that affects a majority of people, particularly during the teenage years. Oil in the skin clogs the tiny pores of the skin. Bacteria collect and feed on the oil, multiplying until an acne sore results. An increase in the skin's oil production during the teen years makes young people particularly susceptible to acne.

Caused by the *Helicobacter pylori* bacterium, an ulcer is a sore in the lining of the stomach or duodenum, a part of the small intestine. Often called peptic ulcers, these infections can produce symptoms of abdominal pain, nausea, vomiting, bloating, and heartburn. Ulcers are treated with drugs such as antacids and antibiotics.

Commonly called pinkeye, conjunctivitis is an inflammation of transparent membranes in the eyeball and eyelid. The staphylococci, pneumococci, and *Haemophilus influenzae* bacteria cause most cases of bacterial pinkeye, which is highly contagious. Conjunctivitis can also result from allergies, viruses, and other causes.

Vaccines and Medicines

The human body produces natural defenses, called antibodies, to fight disease-causing bacteria. To combat the microorganisms' toxins, the body produces anti-toxins. Vaccines and antibiotics are manufactured weapons used to prevent or fight infections. These man-made forms of treatment are prepared using bacteria or their poisonous waste. Vaccines and antitoxin injections are preventive, meaning that they are given when no infection is present in order to protect against a future attack. Antibiotics are used to treat infections that have already set in.

Disease-producing bacteria are used to create vaccines that prevent infections. Given as an injection, a vaccine contains dead or weakened bacteria of the sort the vaccine protects against. The dead bacteria stimulate the human body to react as it would to live bacteria—by producing antibodies. These antibodies protect the individual against the specific kind of bacteria contained in the vaccine. Vaccines protect for a year or longer.

Scientists use bacterial waste products to make antitoxin injections. To make these solutions, the scientist first injects toxins into a living animal. An animal's body produces antitoxins in response to the injected toxins. Then the scientist draws blood from the animal, separates out the serum, and uses it to make an antitoxin for use by humans. Antitoxins work more quickly than vaccines, but they don't last as long—only a few weeks or months.

Antibiotics are drugs that treat bacterial infection. Antibiotics are produced as a secretion by bacteria and other kinds of microorganisms, and this secretion fights germs. Two antibiotics made by bacteria are bacitracin and polymyxin. A group of bacteria called streptomyces, which live in the soil and resemble mold, are used to make many types of antibiotics, including tetracycline and neomycin. Penicillin, made by a mold called *Penicillium notatum*, is a widely used antibiotic.

Along with vaccines, antibiotics are among the most valuable weapons against pathogens and toxins that break through the body's natural defenses. In countries where these medicines are widely available, the incidence of disease decreases dramatically, sometimes disappearing completely.

4 *Beneficial Bacteria*

Although some kinds of bacteria are responsible for infections in humans, plants, and animals, sometimes causing death, bacteria have many valuable uses as well. As mentioned earlier, some of these microbes are used in making foods and fighting diseases. Other bacteria aid in the balance of nature through decay. Numerous other activities of bacteria aid in making human life cleaner, safer, and more enjoyable.

In the Laboratory

Drug makers are always on the lookout for bacteria that may prove useful in fighting diseases. In pharmaceutical laboratories, "bioprospectors" search for microbes to use in new drugs. Much like miners prospecting for gold, these scientists screen large numbers of microbes in order to locate useful ones. Many lifesaving drugs result from this tedious work. For example, some parasitic worm infections can be treated by ivermectin, produced by bacteria that live in soil.

Not all drugs are made by bacteria, of course. Some valuable medicines are created by other organisms in defense against bacteria. For example, a fungus that grows on the Pacific yew tree produces a substance to fight disease-causing bacteria. Scientists found that this drug, called paclitaxel, fights certain kinds of cancer, too.

Many kinds of bacteria develop resistance or immunity to antibiotics that previously killed them. For example, staphylococcus is a common bacterium responsible for staph infections. It has developed a resistance to certain antibiotics. Bacteria's ability to adapt drives scientists to search for newer drugs that will be effective, at least for a time. Viruses known as bacteriophages attack and kill specific bacteria. Scientists are turning to viruses in search of new means of combating bacterial infections. *E. coli* bacteria, for example, fall victim to certain viruses.

The study of bacteria in laboratories results in more than just drugs to fight

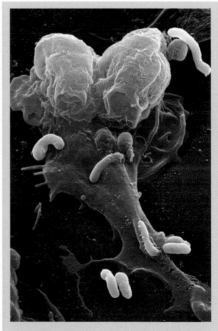

A macrophage white blood cell (shown in brown) engulfs *Heliobacter pylori* bacteria (in yellow) by extending itself to surround and capture the bacteria.

infections. Bacteria are used to rid crops of pests naturally. Natural pesticides called bioinsecticides repel pests or kill them outright. For instance, the *Bacillus thuringiensis* bacterium kills pests on crops and kills mosquitoes. Harmless to humans, it is a safe alternative to chemical pesticide and is used world-wide. Some bioinsecticides are mixed with cornstarch in a special process that prepares them to be spread on crops by crop-dusting aircraft.

Genetic Engineering

Like all living cells, bacteria contain hereditary information. This hereditary information is called DNA. It determines the cell's traits and activities. When the bacterium splits, the DNA determines that the new cells have the same or similar traits as the first cell. DNA is comprised of chromosomes that carry genes. Floating around inside the cell are also small pieces of DNA called plasmids.

Scientists discovered that they could take plasmids from one bacterium and put them into another. This action changed the traits of the altered bacterium. Scientists also found that they could cut up the DNA in the chromosome and join the pieces with DNA from a different kind of bacteria. The new DNA carried some traits from both bacteria. These activities are known as genetic engineering.

Scientists took what they learned from working with bacteria and applied it to other living organisms. Genetic engineers learned how to move genes from one animal to another and even from an animal or human to a plant. They modified fruits and vegetables to produce more desirable strains. In the mid-1980s, they began cloning organisms, making genetic copies of them. Scientists used the fertilized eggs of sheep, cows, rabbits,

Dolly the cloned sheep made headlines when she was born in 1996. She died of a lung infection at a fairly young age in 2003, which raised fears about the health problems of clones.

and other animals to make clones. In early 1997, a sheep named Dolly became famous as the first complex organism cloned from the cell of an adult. This scientific work, which amazed people all over the world, grew out of the original work with bacterial DNA.

In Industry

Besides being important to laboratory research, bacteria are important in real-world applications

An oil-skimming operation cleans up part of the *Exxon Valdez* oil spill in April 1989. Besides skimming, people cleaning up oil spills can also use chemicals to break down the oil, but this may kill marine life. Many oil spills are now cleaned by using fertilizer to encourage the growth of oil-eating bacteria.

such as mining. Called biomining, a process using *Thiobacillus ferrooxidans* bacteria extracts metals from ore. These microbes get their energy from combining oxygen with inorganic material such as minerals. In doing so, the bacteria release acid that washes metals out of ore. Miners remove copper from ore using *Thiobacillus ferrooxidans* bacteria. Gold, too, is separated from ore using biomining.

Thanks to genetic engineering, a kind of bacteria has been developed for the purpose of eating oil. Oil spills like the *Exxon Valdez* oil tanker spill in 1989 coat huge areas of water with oil. As a result, vast numbers of fish, birds, and other wildlife suffer or die. The 11 million-gallon (41.6 million-liter) *Exxon Valdez* spill created an oil slick covering nearly 100 square miles (260 square kilometers) off the coast of Alaska. For some bacteria, this oil is a feast. In the early 1970s, scientists genetically created bacteria that could eat oil. To clean up an oil slick, sawdust is sprinkled over it. The oil soaks into the sawdust, forming globs that sink to the bottom. Here bacteria devour the oil, decomposing it and making it harmless. Another method of cleaning an oil slick is sprinkling it with clay. Like the sawdust, the clay absorbs the oil, only it does not sink. Bacteria decompose these clumps of oil-soaked clay.

In science, medicine, industry, and everyday human life, bacteria continue to play vital roles. Perhaps more than any other living organism, bacteria determine the course of human, animal, and plant life on this planet.

Glossary

aerobic   Living in the presence of oxygen.

anaerobic   Living in the absence of oxygen.

antibiotic   A drug made to destroy living organisms, such as bacteria, that cause infection.

antibody   A protein produced by white blood cells in an immune response to fight organisms such as bacteria that cause infection.

antitoxin   An antibody produced to fight a toxin.

bacillus (plural: bacilli)   A bacterium with a rodlike shape.

cell   The smallest unit of independent life. All living organisms are made up of one or more cells.

chromosome   The DNA-containing particle within a cell.

clone   An organism that is an exact genetic match to its parent.

coccus (plural: cocci)   A bacteria with a spherical shape.

DNA (deoxyribonucleic acid)   DNA is made up of genes, the hereditary information for a cell.

epidemic   An outbreak of a disease affecting a large portion of a population at once.

flagellum (plural: flagella) A long whiplike tail on some protozoans, including some bacteria. Flagella provide a means of movement.

gene A tiny part of a chromosome that holds hereditary information for a cell.

immunity Resistance to infection or poison.

nitrogen fixation The process whereby certain bacteria in the soil take nitrogen gas from the air and convert it to nitrates, which are necessary to plant growth.

pasteurization A process whereby liquids or foods are heated to specific temperatures for certain lengths of time to kill microscopic organisms.

pathogen A disease-causing bacterium or other agent.

plasmid A particle of DNA within a bacterium cell.

spirillum (plural: spirilla) A coil-shaped bacterium cell. Cells with this shape are also called spirochetes.

toxin Poisonous waste material produced by a bacterium.

vaccine A solution made from weakened or dead disease-causing organisms (such as bacteria and viruses). Injected into a person, a vaccine causes the body to develop antibodies.

For More Information

American Public Health Association
800 I Street NW
Washington, DC 20001-3710
(202) 777-2742
e-mail: comments@apha.org
Web site: http://www.apha.org

Centers for Disease Control and Prevention
1600 Clifton Road
Atlanta, GA 30333
(404) 639-3534
(800) 311-3435
Web site: http://www.cdc.gov

National Institutes of Health (NIH)
9000 Rockville Pike
Bethesda, MD 20892
(301) 496-4000
e-mail: NIHInfo@OD.NIH.GOV
Web site: http://www.nih.gov

Hotlines

National Immunization Hotlines
(800) 232-2522 (English)
(800) 232-0233 (Spanish)

National STD Hotline
(800) 227-8922

Traveler's Health Hotline
(877) FYI-TRIP (394-8747)

Web Sites

Due to the changing nature of Internet links, the Rosen Publishing Group, Inc., has developed an online list of Web sites related to the subject of this book. This site is updated regularly. Please use this link to access the list:

http://www.rosenlinks.com/germ/bact

For Further Reading

Biddle, Wayne. *A Field Guide to Germs*. New York: Henry Holt, 1995.

Bottone, Frank G., Jr. "Bacteria Are Everywhere (Kingdom Prokaryotae)." *The Science of Life: Projects and Principles for Beginning Biologists*. Chicago: Chicago Review Press, 2001.

Corzine, Phyllis. *The Black Death*. San Diego: Lucent Books, 1997.

Edwards, Gabrielle I. "Bacteria and Viruses." *Biology the Easy Way*. Third edition. Hauppauge, NY: Barron's, 2000.

Friedman, B. Ellen. *Bacteria*. Mankato, MN: Creative Education, 1997.

Hyde, Margaret O., and Elizabeth H. Forsythe. *The Disease Book: A Kid's Guide*. New York: Walker and Company, 1997.

Nardo, Don. *Germs*. San Diego: KidHaven Press, 2002.

Snedden, Robert. *The Benefits of Bacteria*. Chicago: Heinemann, 2000.

Snedden, Robert. *The World of the Cell: Life on a Small Scale*. Chicago: Heinemann, 2003.

Bibliography

Biddle, Wayne. *A Field Guide to Germs*. New York: Henry Holt, 1995.

Eberhart-Phillips, Jason. *Outbreak Alert: Responding to the Increasing Threat of Infectious Diseases*. Oakland, CA: New Harbinger Publications, 2000.

Facklam, Howard, and Margery Facklam. *Bacteria*. New York: Twenty-first Century Books, 1994.

Farrell, Jeanette. *Invisible Enemies: Stories of Infectious Disease*. New York: Farrar, Straus & Giroux, 1998.

Patent, Dorothy Hinshaw. *Bacteria: How They Affect Other Living Things*. New York: Holiday House, 1980.

Snedden, Robert. *The Benefits of Bacteria*. Chicago: Heinemann, 2000.

Index

A
aerobes, 15, 21
anaerobes, 15, 20
  photosynthesis and,
    18–19
antibiotics, 31, 32, 33, 35
antibodies, 32
antitoxins, 32–33
asexual reproduction, 12

B
bacteria
  discovery of, 4
  food of, 17–19
  habitats of, 14–17
  human defenses against,
    27–28, 32
  movement of, 11–12
  parasitic, 18
  reproduction of, 12–13
  size of, 8–9
  spoilage and, 22–23
  structure of, 7–8
  thermophilic, 23
  types of, 9–12
bacteriology, 4
binary fission, 12
biomining, 38
botulin, 24

C
cholera, 6

conjugation, 12–13
conjunctivitis/pinkeye, 10,
    27, 31

D
decomposition, 19–21
diplococcus, 10
diseases, 26–31
DNA, 8, 13, 36

E
epidemic, 6
  Yersinia pestis, 6
Escherichia coli, 16, 35
Exxon Valdez spill, 38–39

F
fermentation, 24–25
food, canning of, 23, 24

G
genetic engineering,
    36–37, 38

H
hygiene, 25–26

I
immune system, 28

46

About the Author

Lesli J. Favor received her B.A. in English from the University of Texas at Arlington, and then earned her M.A. and Ph.D. from the University of North Texas. She has also written *Francisco de Coronado* and *Martin Van Buren*. She now lives with her husband, Stephen, in Dallas.

Photo Credits